to my
DADDY

from ....

I love making sandcastles with you.

Finish this sandcastle and decorate it with shells and flags.

I did this picture
of us together.

Draw you and Daddy here.

I love helping you
in the garden.

Fill the garden with plants and flowers.

I love playing games with you.

Draw Daddy's favourite game.

I love bathtime with you.

Fill the bathroom with bubbles.

I love looking at
the stars with you.

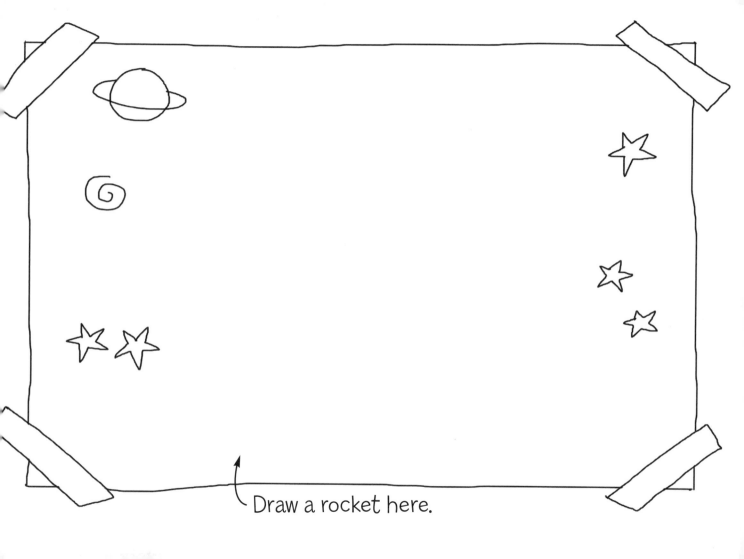

Draw a rocket here.

I love seeing you
after school.

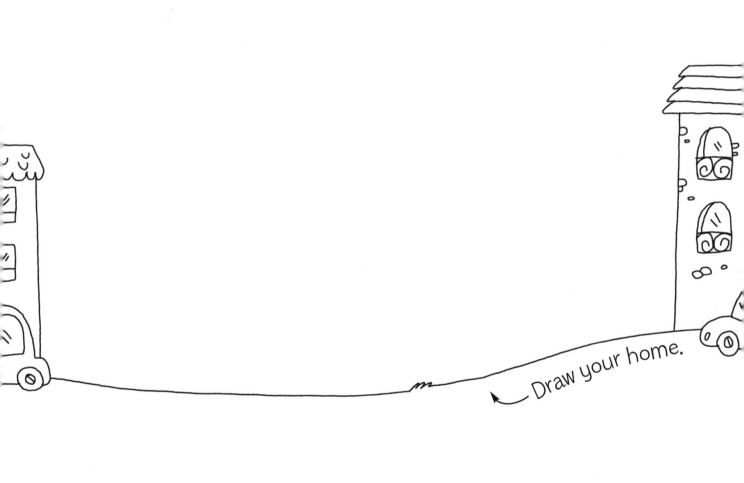

Draw your home.

I love going swimming
with you.

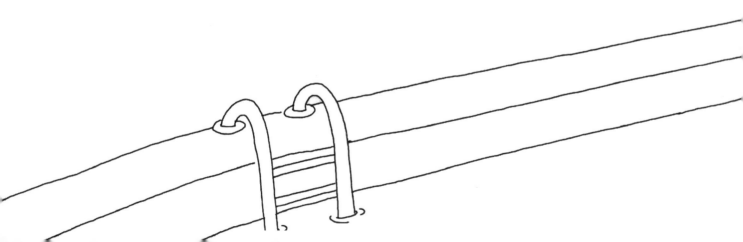

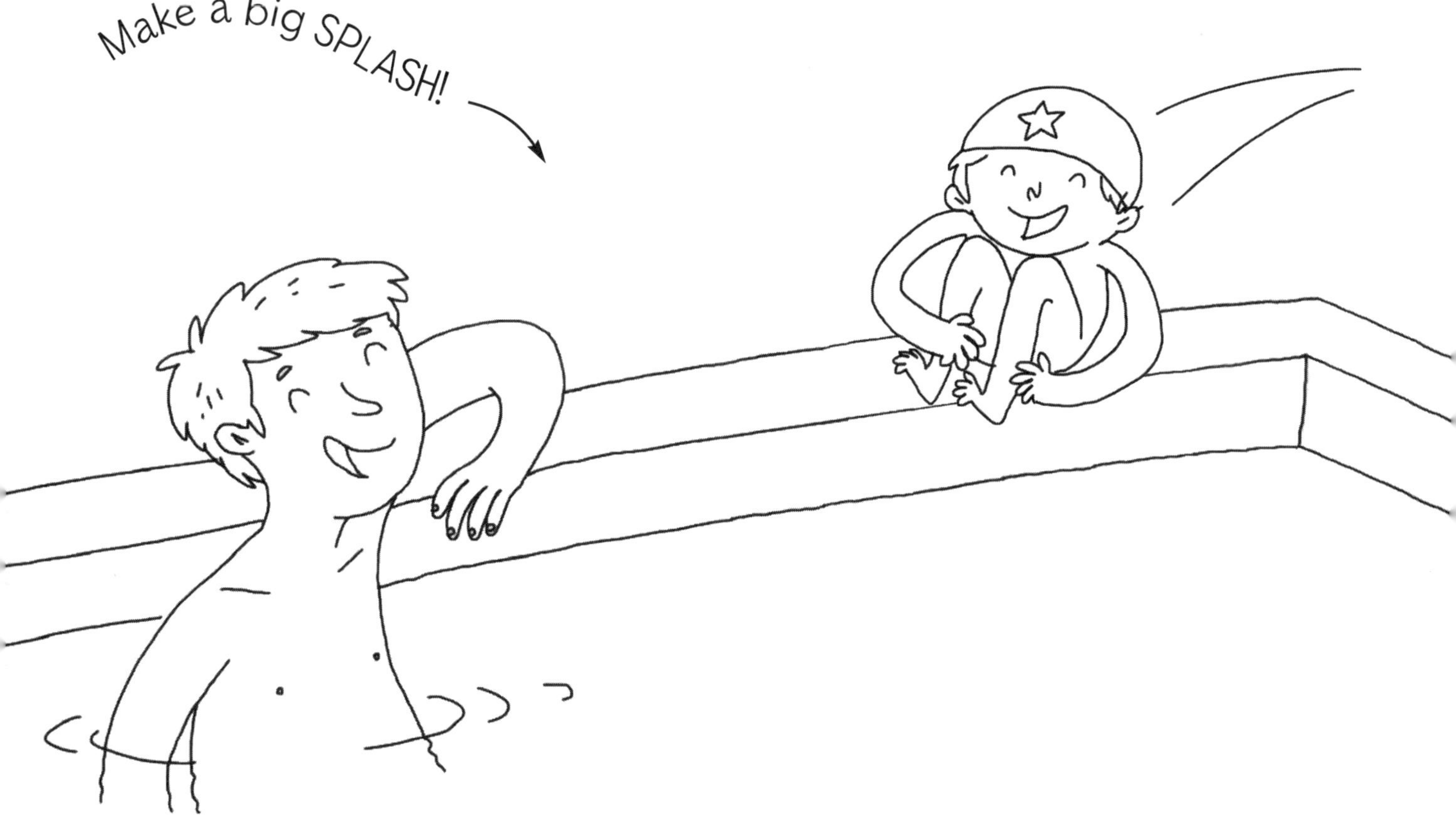
Make a big SPLASH!

I love races with you.

Draw yourself racing Daddy. Who is winning?

I put your favourite topping
on this pizza.

Draw Daddy's favourite topping.

I love it when you
tuck me in at night.

What's outside your bedroom window?

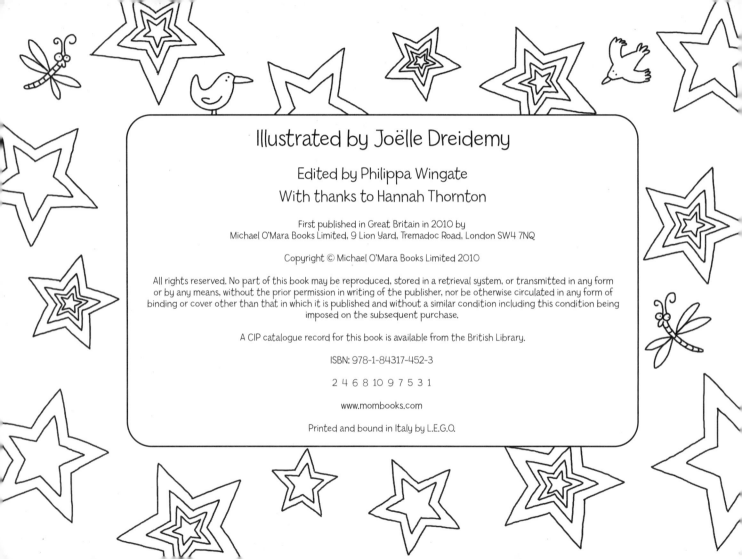

Illustrated by Joëlle Dreidemy

Edited by Philippa Wingate
With thanks to Hannah Thornton

First published in Great Britain in 2010 by
Michael O'Mara Books Limited, 9 Lion Yard, Tremadoc Road, London SW4 7NQ

A CIP catalogue record for this book is available from the British Library.

ISBN: 978-1-84317-452-3

2 4 6 8 10 9 7 5 3 1

www.mombooks.com

Printed and bound in Italy by L.E.G.O.